A Touch of God's Grace

To: Kate thanks!
May the grace of God
Bless You with Joy. &
Peace Love You, Suzy ♥

Entering A New Dimension

A Touch of God's Grace

Chaplain Luz N. Rivera

Editing by Spill Some Ink

Published by Spill Some Ink at Lulu Publishing

Copyright 2023

First Edition

Library of Congress Cataloging – in – Publication Data available on file.

ISBN 978 1 387 45133 3

Scripture references are from the Holy Bible: English Standard Version, King James Version, and Contemporary English Version.

Published in the United States of America

Acknowledgements

I would like to acknowledge my family. First, to my father Domingo and my mother, María, who are resting in heaven. Then to my brothers, Edwin and Francisco, my sister, Hilda, and my children, Willie and Janie Luz. Then to my grandchildren, Kaitlyn, Jazmine, Blayze, Ciara, Desiree, Mariah and Misael and my great-grandchildren, Katai, Rheyna and Esme Luz, my niece, Mary and my nephews, Robert, Joe, and Carlos. They all are my greatest treasures in this world that cause me to laugh many times and have been my greatest motivation. I continually pray and call on God for His mercy and grace for each of them.

I also thank God and acknowledge true friends and real sisters that became special angels for me in my life. Pastor Leah Payne who referred me to Pastor Paula Jackson and her editing and publishing company, *Spill Some Ink*. Because of God's grace and these ladies, I was able to bring this vision to fruition.

Dedication

I dedicate this book with all my love to the Holy Spirit of God. You are my counselor, my redeemer, my advocate and my friend. You have been my constant traveling companion during my life. You were there through the valleys and also the times when I traveled through some exciting experiences in my life.

You have guided me and directed my path into the arms of many Godly servants, brothers and sisters who were sent to help me understand the amazing and forgiving love of Abba Father.

Therefore, because of the Touch of Grace of the Holy Spirit, my faith continues to grow through the years and today I can testify and believe that there is nothing impossible because the Holy Spirit is always for us, fighting to show us the incomparable and unconditional love of our Eternal Father.

He who carries the Word of God

is building the Kingdom of God in the earth,
with the mercies and grace of the Holy Spirit.

Preface

This book is designated for you who need to know the touch of God's grace. I feel so humbled to hear His command, by the voice of God Himself, to write my experiences and the words spoken to me while He has been guiding my journey in this world. This journey has been very joyous on some occasions, but also troubling in other ways.

Sometimes, there has been laughter and thanksgiving and also sadness, loneliness and screams of pain, yet still I thank the Lord with humility and I remember His words: "Rejoice always, pray continually, give thanks in all circumstances, for this is the will of God for you, in Christ Jesus." I. Thessalonians 5: 16-18

I hope that this book will be a great blessing to all who read it and are in need of a touch of God's grace. His grace may help you to come closer to his divine presence; to know the heart of God and His plan for your life.

It is my goal that through this book, as you read and meditate in His grace, my friend, that you will be uplifted with words of encouragement and hope, that will motivate you to continue walking in your journey with the help of the only one who can help us, that is Jesus Christ, our friend, our Redeemer.

In Service to our Savior,

Chaplain Luz

Behold, I will do a new thing, now it shall spring forth, shall ye not know it? I will make a way in the wilderness, and rivers in the desert. Isaiah 43: 19

Why did God name this book, "Touch of God's Grace"? Because God, our Creator, still continues to write and create new things every day for us to see His grace and to lift up our eyes to see what He is doing for each of us as individuals and as a community where He has established us. God is here with us! Praise His name! He has never forsaken us. Through the years, we are beginning to feel that Jesus is coming back again soon for His people that believe in Him and who have waited with passion to see Him face to face. Hallelujah! Let us lift up our eyes and let us come closer to His presence today because His mercies are new every day! Arise people of God and shine because the Lord has risen and is upon you as He promised in the Holy Bible. (Isaiah 60: 1 – 3.)

The things that eyes have not seen are the things that God has decreed for all to see soon. His promises are being fulfilled. Lift up your eyes to the mountains of Jehovah and He will guide you. You will see the earth reborn and enlivened and the glory of God will shine. Seek today His presence and the touch of God's grace will cover you and you will be renewed. He will change your sorrow into dancing and you will praise His blessed name every day of your life that He has given you upon the earth that He created for you and for me.

The LORD is my shepherd; I shall not want. He maketh me to lie down in green pastures: he leadeth me beside the still waters. He restoreth my soul: he leadeth me in the paths of righteousness for his name's sake. Yea, though I walk through the valley of the shadow of death, I will fear no evil: for thou art with me; thy rod and thy staff they comfort me. Thou preparest a table before me in the presence of mine enemies: thou anointest my head with oil; my cup runneth over. Surely goodness and mercy shall follow me all the days of my life: and I will dwell in the house of the LORD forever. Psalm 23

The Lord says do not delay! Do not stop! It is necessary that you continue doing the works of the Lord. Serve the Lord and in everything you do, it is not for others to see, but only to please God. You are not wasting your time when you pray, praise fast or serve Him in any way.

You are giving God glory and honor. Continue your praise from your heart, like a sweet fragrance. When this happens, God spills His love and His mercy over your life and your loved one's lives. Preach! Run with the Word of God and one day soon we will be in front of Him, to see His face and to live with Him forever. Hallelujah!

Jesus answered and said unto him, Verily, verily, I say unto thee, Except a man be born again, he cannot see the kingdom of God. Nicodemus saith unto him, How can a man be born when he is old? can he enter the second time into his mother's womb, and be born? Jesus answered, Verily, verily, I say unto thee, Except a man be born of water and of the Spirit, he cannot enter into the kingdom of God. That which is born of the flesh is flesh; and that which is born of the Spirit is spirit. Marvel not that I said unto thee, Ye must be born again. The wind bloweth where it pleaseth, and thou hearest the sound thereof, but canst not tell whence *it cometh, and whither it goeth: so is every one that is born of the Spirit. St. John 3: 3-8*

Praises to the one who lives for the centuries of centuries – King of Kings, Lord of Lords – Jesus Christ.

Blessed is the one you discipline, LORD, the one you teach from your law; you grant them relief from days of trouble, till a pit is dug for the wicked. For the LORD will not reject his people; he will never forsake his inheritance. Judgment will again be founded on righteousness, and all the upright in heart will follow it.   Psalms 94: 12 – 15

We give thanks to God for His forgiving grace and all His patience. What would it be like for us, if it wasn't for His forgiving grace that sustains us in the midst of our difficulties and trials? Our trials are many and we would think that we have been forsaken. But the Bible says that Jesus will always be with us, even in the end of our days. His promises are true and not a lie. Nevertheless, in His timing, God shows up and we cross through the valley of difficulties, sickness, and even loneliness. We sing the song of victory that Moses sang with the people when they crossed the Red Sea. They sang songs of joy and thanksgiving for deliverance when they thought nothing was able to save them. They were joyous when they realized that the Lord had not forsaken them. Hallelujah!

He replied, "Because you have so little faith. Truly I tell you, if you have faith as small as a mustard seed, you can say to this mountain, 'Move from here to there,' and it will move. Nothing will be impossible for you." Matthew 17:20

When we open our hearts to Jesus, the kingdom of heaven becomes like a small mustard seed. Jesus wants us to be like a small mustard seed. A small seed enters into our hearts and as time passes, while we listen to God day by day, that seed starts to transform you.

Faith is the beginning of an action and power. When we put all our strength into reaching a goal, we are manifesting faith because we show hope in something we cannot see. Faith is the conviction of things not seen. (Hebrews 11:1) The conviction that comes from faith, that is given by God and comes when we understand that God is the creator of all things and nothing escapes from His hand.

We must give thanks to the Lord every day for His forgiving grace that sustains us in the midst of difficulties and trials, when they are many.

And teaching them to obey everything I have commanded you. And surely I am with you always, to the very end of the age.
Matthew 28:20

The storm is sent to strengthen you. Jesus pushed you towards the storm to bless you! One of the most precious promises that Jesus has given us is, "I am with you every day, even until the end of the world." How conscious are you of this reality, of this visible truth? When hard circumstances come to your life, God is with us every day, even unto the end of this world. Every day!

The world is searching for peace, tranquility and security. Even Christians who confess to have faith in God are looking for these things. The question is, where can we find peace and security? Science promises deliverance from trouble, but is the contrary.

We are consistently entangled in troubles and difficult circumstances. We need peace and we need to calm our nerves and feelings.

Jesus said, "My peace I leave with you, my peace I give unto you, not as the world gives, I give unto you. (John 14:24) I have told you these things so that in me you will have peace. In this world you will have trouble, but take heart. I have overcome the world. (John 16:33) There is no other place when you can be and feel secure, except in Jesus.

Many are the afflictions of the righteous, but the Lord delivered Him out of them all.   *Psalms 34:19*

I have learned through all my battles, to keep silent before Jehovah and to learn the lesson behind my struggles. Is there something that happened that the Lord Almighty has not permitted with divine purpose? Meditating in the word of God these days, I have learned to suffer for being a Christian and a follower of Jesus Christ.

Beloved, do not think it strange concerning the fiery trial, which is to try you, as though some strange thing happened to you; but rejoice to the extent that you partake of Christ's sufferings, that when His glory is revealed, you may also be glad with exceeding joy.   I Peter 4: 12 – 13

We are om the center of the will of God and there is a battle that we will have to suffer through, but there are also victories that we will be the conqueror, a weight of glory that will glorify God in our lives.

We will have to trust God, no matter what comes our way. Wait, because He will take care of us and we will arrive at the finish line at the specific time appointed by God. He is faithful. Wait on His promises. He will fulfill them all. One day, everything will make sense. God to the one who lives forevermore. Hallelujah!

Behold, I am the Lord, the God of all flesh. Is there anything too hard for me? Jeremiah 32: 26 - 27

I write what is written in the Bible and I am sure what I am writing because I will be drawn myself when all the circumstances of life come. In other words, today I write for you and for me. We tend to see our own problems and when someone else tells us their problems, it seems like their problems and circumstances are not as great as our own.

Is there anything too difficult for me? Certainly for God there is nothing impossible or difficult. He made light from darkness. He made visible from the invisible. He made what exists from that which did not exist. God calls the things that are not, as though they are. There is nothing too difficult for God.

This is the time to ask God to forgive us. Think about that big problem that you have in the present or in the past. That problem that keeps you in fear and makes you waste time during the day and even during the night when you are unable to sleep. Ask God to forgive you. The problem is not that big because the word says that there is no problem too big for God.

You have to focus on your storm. Ask God to forgive you and faith in God will come over you. You will look at Jesus and say, "Lord, let me walk on water, as you walked on water." The water would not sink and will keep you afloat.

Let us pray:

Lord, I receive this word. May God enter my heart. I confess that you are mighty Jesus; that you are powerful. You walked on the waters and you also command me to walk on the waters. God forgive me for making my circumstances bigger than you. Thank you Lord! I receive faith. I put out all bitterness and doubt. This I pray in Jesus' name. Amen!

But as it is written: Eye has not seen, nor ear heard, Nor have entered into the heart of man The things which God has prepared for those who love Him.   I Corinthians 2:9

There are some people who consider heaven a mere state of the spirit, or a region of dreams and fantasies. Other people think that it is a definitive region in the universal geography, where the spirits of death move playing harps. There are others that describe heaven like a place where redeemers fly with bird wings. These and others ideas lack biblical support and are responsible for a growing indifference for the future life.

The Bible defines heaven as a place. In John 14, Jesus professes, "I go to prepare a place for you." But what kind of place is heaven? The Apostle Paul attempted to describe it, but subsequently confessed his limitations by saying, *"Eyes have not seen, nor* ears heard, neither has it entered into the hearts of man, the things which God has prepared for them that love Him." The imagination most fertile can conceive the magnitude and the excellence of what the Eternal Father is preparing for His children.

A place where He will wipe away every tear from their eyes and death shall be no more; neither shall there be mourning nor crying, no pain anymore for the former things have passed away. Revelation 21:4

These disabilities in describing the wonders that are awaiting us, are due to the fact that there is a track of unsupportive comparison about the things that we know. God affirmed: Behold, I will make all things new! Revelation 21:5.

This declaration is better understood when related with the description that the Lord gave us by St. John. I saw a new heaven and a new earth, for the first heaven and the first earth were passed away and there was no more sea. And I, John, saw the Holy city, the new Jerusalem, coming down from God out *of heaven, prepared as a bride adorned for her husband.*

The paradise of God will be a place of interminable joy and creative activity.

Here I am! I stand as the door and knock. If any man hears my voice and opens the door, I will come in and eat with them, and they with me. To the one who is victorious, I will give the right to sit with me on my throne, just as I was victorious and sat down with my Father on His throne. Whomever has ears, let them hear what the spirit says to the churches. Revelation 3:20 – 22

All that have ears, listen to what will happen to those that see the Lord at the door of their hearts, calling with love and mercy. Allow this day, the Lord to enter, to eat with you and be a victorious person. The best is about to happen to any child of God that listens to His voice and does not harden their heart. This is better than anything that this world could offer us. There is nothing better! Glory to God!

But they that wait upon the Lord, shall renew their strength; they shall mount up with wings as eagles; they shall run and not be weary; and they shall walk and not faint.
Isaiah 40:31

All throughout the day, I meditated on this verse. The Lord gave me a vision of being in the body of an eagle, sitting in my house, waiting for a call, a letter or a visit from someone that could help me pass my Jordan. I saw how new feathers began to grow out, in place of the old, worn out feathers. These new feathers were full of energy that would help me to rise again, to face the final stage of the most important flight, over the heights with God. The Lord showed me that precisely now, many are facing tiredness, fatigue and are in a valley of decisions. He wants to help us to wait on Him with patience.

It is possible to walk again without fainting; it is possible to run again and not be weary and it is possible to mount up in flight as an eagle, over adverse situations as though we were young and full of energy. The Lord is asking you today, "Is there anything too difficult for me?"

When we feel rejuvenated in His strength, we are able to fly over the trials and storms in our lives, just like an eagle, towards a new higher dimension that will take us face to face to King Jesus. In our flight, He wants us to have a divine encounter, and to embrace Him and depend on him like we have never done before. Glory to God!

How many of you would like to fly towards the Lord in this new dimension to embrace Him? It is possible, saith the Lord!

Because of the vision, I bring to you this exhortation to show you how we can wait on God with patience.

Don't try to accelerate the creative process. It is better to learn how to wait.

That way, you can accept that He knows how to do it better.

It is a stupid intent to open a bud; vain thing trying to help it out.

You will destroy the beautiful butterfly, for everything that has been created, has a conceived plan. God has a timed plan that must be respected to fulfill its objective. The time in God is not lost. Our God is not in a rush.

From the ant to the star, He sees His wise and beautiful footprint to provoke our smiles.

Do not be impatient. Wait and trust in Him.

God will work wisely in our lives, faithfully and you will never regret it.

If you long for His blessings, be patient and live attentive, looking for His orientation, and you will have the answer at the right time.

Do not pay attention to people's comments, that you have lost your timing. To the contrary: wait!

It is necessary to be strengthened. We are the sheep near our great Master.

Our worries are in vain. God works according to His plans for our profit! Amen.

But be ye doers of the word, and not hearers only, deceiving yourselves. James 1:22

Show me how!!! These are words that I have heard many times. On each conference, it's been told to the writers, "Do not tell, show it!"

The Bible shows us how to live abundantly. Jesus came not only to talk, but also to show how much God loves us. The beginning of Jesus was by being born and by living in the same condition as we all live. He showed us how to love and how to take care of each other. When He talked to the people from Samaria and when they became the heroes of their stories, Jesus taught us how to be kind to people that are not pleasant to us. In Gethsemane, Jesus showed us how to be obedient. On the cross, Jesus taught us how to love, and in the resurrection, how to be victorious.

Jesus said many beautiful words and he invited us to proclaim His message, but the message will have more power if it is shown by his disciples, how to be kind to people that are not pleasant to us.

TALK ABOUT YOUR FAITH AND SHOW IT

Yea, though I walk through the valley of the shadow of death, I will fear no evil, for thou art with me; thy rod and thy staff they comfort me. Psalms 23:4

The fear of death is natural in all men, especially when you are living in the spring days of your life. Even those that do not suffer fear, they may feel depressed about the possibility of a sudden encounter with death, which brings with its cold hands the black passport for the journey to the world of silence. Fear may intensify because of certain diseases that generally precede death.

When David Hume, the philosopher, realized the proximity of death he declared in distress, "I felt frightened and confused when I saw what kind of abyss I faced because of my philosophical thinking. Where am I? Who am I? Where am I going?. I started to perceive that I had found myself surrounded by impenetrable darkness."

This was the thinking of a man that had not met God. One who had lived without faith and hope for tomorrow. However, a man who has faith, a man that has encountered God and one who has studied his word will live a completely opposite experience. This man is not fearful of death. He knows that this life is only the stage for a glorious tomorrow, together with our Creator. He is not fearful of the grave because he has certainty that he was not created just for this time, but for all eternity. With brilliant trust, accompanied the Psalmist of Israel, he was inspired to speak this truth

"Yeah, though I walk through the valley of the shadow of death, I will fear no evil, for though art with me."

Those that desire to enjoy the peace of the Spirit must learn to tear down fear, with the confidence that our life is hidden in the mighty hands of our Creator. <u>For in Him we live, and move and have our being</u>. (Acts 17:28) <u>If we live, we live for the Lord, and if we die, we die for the Lord; so whether we live or die, we belong to the Lord</u>. (Rom. 14: 8-10)

Those who believe in Christ do not fear going through the valley of the shadow of death because on the other side of the grave, there is resurrection and the celestial home where there will be no more death, nor tears, nor pain. (Rev. 21:4)

Come unto me all ye that labor and are heavy laden and I will give you rest. Matthew 11:28

Anxiety is a bad thing. It steals the interior peace, weakens the physical energies, disturbs sleep and produces stress and anguish. To be worried affects the blood circulation, the heart, the glands and all of the nervous system. I never met anyone who died because of excessive physical work, but to the contrary, I met many people who have died the victim of uncontrolled anxiety.

70% of all patients that come for medical attention could be healed by themselves if they just controlled their anxiety and fear. I'm not saying that his condition is imaginary. Their ailments are as real as a toothache and sometimes more serious. But I refer to their conditions as nervous exhaustion, gastric ulcers, cardiac disturbances, insomnia and even paralysis.

The modern ships have their helmets divided in compartments that can be separated from each other by gates. If the water penetrates one of them, it can prevent them from invading the ship and sinking it.

The same way our days must be separated in such a way that the anguish of yesterday and the insecurity of tomorrow does not disturb today. God created natural gates, separating the days; between those gates and the nights. To know how to sleep free of worries, fatigue, and the cares of this life, is an indispensable element for our full existence. God is the craftsman of our future.

Let's take to Him all of our weights and cares. Nothing is too big for Him to bear. Anything that somehow affects our peace, no matter how small, does not mean that God cannot see it. No disaster can happen to the smallest of His children; no anxiety can rob the soul without God, our Great Counselor, taking immediate interest in it. Because our trust in God is the effective antidote against the worries of our lives. Come unto Him all ye that labor and are heavy laden, because He will give you rest. Amen.

In the multitude of my thoughts within me thy comforts delight my soul.   *Psalms 94:19*

The anxieties that conspire against our mental health are often caused by the imagination. In the hillside of a mountain in the state of Colorado, there was the remains of a gigantic tree. This tree kept itself standing up for 400 years. It was just a shrub when Cristobal Colon disembarked in Santa Domingo. The tree was in the middle of its growth when pilgrims established themselves in Plymouth in 1620.

During its long existence, it was touched 14 times by the sudden and devastating actions of the electrical rays of lightening. Many windstorms went over this tree. However, for 400 years it survived the fury of nature. Then one day it was attacked by an army of small white ants, annihilating it. The ants penetrated across the thickness of the bark of the tree, and destroyed gradually its interior vitality through small and constant attacks.

A giant of the jungle that did not weaken with age, that resisted the actions of the electrical rays and the impetus of the windstorms, fell finally as a result of the insidious action of the small ants.

Are not we, maybe, like that tree? We resisted with notable energy the storms of life. Some other times permit our minds to be devoured by the small cares and the imaginary anxieties that maim our physical energy and weaken our spiritual vigor....

If we desire to prevent the cares of life to maim our physical vigor, we must live fully every day, not allowing our failures of yesterday and the uncertain expectations of tomorrow to invade the day today. Jesus said, Therefore, do not worry about tomorrow, for tomorrow will worry about itself. Each day has enough trouble of its own.

When the cares of this life depress our being, we must trust like David did, in the comfort that comes from the Lord because the multitude of our thoughts, your comfort Oh Lord delights our soul. Hallelujah.

Fear thou not; for I am with thee: be not dismayed; for I am thy God: I will strengthen thee; yea, I will help thee; yea, I will uphold thee with the right hand of my righteousness.   Isaiah 41:10

This is one of my favorite scriptures. It can be found in the Old Testament and has helped me so much through the years.

This verse was given to Israel but also to all of God's children today. Many times we say, "Don't be afraid; there will be better days." This is a human saying to encourage those who are discouraged, but God says, "Do not be afraid because I am with you. This is a good motivation to not be afraid. God offers us divine healing and divine deliverance. How can a person be afraid knowing that God is with you? Not if you know who God is. We cannot fear if we have known the great love that God had for all who believe in Him and search for Him in prayer.

Even before I knew the whole Gospel, I did not cry or ask God for His help, but I would open the Bible to the scriptures, like this one, and then I would fall on my knees in His presence and say, "My God, I am so glad that you are with me and that you are my God. You strengthen me and sustain me with your right hand of justice and I do not have to be in fear. You have told me that I must not be confused." This way, you can smile even in your darkest hours of life.

It is good to have friends that support us during our trials and tribulations. But the Lord, He is always with us. He is our Helper. For you who are discouraged, crying and saying, "Oh God, help us," I want to tell you that God already helped us because He is a God of compassion and He descends to our level. If God be for us, who can be against us? (Romans 8:31

This should be our confession when we face our adversaries. God is certainly for us! He is not against us. All that you ask in prayer believing, you will receive it. He said it and He does not lie. He is a God of truth and His mercies are new every day! Hallelujah.

For thou shalt be his witness unto all men of what thou hast seen and heard. Acts 22:15

The following verse of scripture captured my attention. "Be doers of the word, and not hearers only, deceiving your own selves. (James 1:22) Even though I am familiar with the bible teachings, I have been negligent in obeying the truth that I say I believe.

One specific day, I promised the Lord that I would be a doer of what His word says about making disciples. For too many Christians it seems difficult to talk to others about Jesus. In certain situations, we fear to say or to do something incorrect. We forget that we are called to be witnesses of what we have see and of what we know. The key is sincerity and obedience. Faithfulness is our responsibility and the results align with God and with His holy word.

When there is a unique opportunity to testify, God is not waiting for eloquence, but He is waiting for our obedience. In Christ, we have the greatest treasure that we could ever know. So why do we hesitate to share Him with others? There is no bigger honor than to be the instrument that guides another person to the glorious light of the knowledge of God.

In the movement of God, time moves forward with torrents of peace, goodness, and love. Justice and equality belongs to the Lord. He is our strength and our hope forever. Hurry up! Serve the Lord without delay. Be thankful of His goodness and His favor.

God is listening to our call, our clamor, our subtle prayers and our praise. Lord, we will exalt you as long as we have life! We will glorify you! Oh God, we will immerse ourselves in you forever.

Let's pray:

Our wonderful and mighty God, through your Holy Spirit, strengthen us with your power to testify in the name of Jesus. Give us a baptism of love that allows all barriers and all fear to fall down. Give us the power to serve you every minute and in every place. We thank you for your underserving love. Amen.

Wisdom From God

Lot, Abraham's nephew, ended his life like a prisoner of the enemy because he decided to live in a land he thought was good, but found that it was surrounded by evil people. He chose what he thought was best for him, instead of choosing the best according to the will of God.

How many times will people walk away from the umbrella of protection that God provides, which is far from God's goodness? How many times will people choose what they believe is better for their lives without asking for God's wisdom and direction? How many times have we done it? The fact that we have spent time with God does not make us immune to this issue. We think that we know what is God's will in certain situations because it was His will in times past. However, what was good in times past may not be God's will today. We need to continually ask God for His wisdom and direction.

We cannot begin to imagine how many times God's wisdom has saved us or caused us to avoid something painful. This is why we cannot live without God's wisdom.

We need to pray. Ask God to give us wisdom in everything that we do. Please help us God to walk in your wisdom each day.

Ten Good Reasons Why We Need to Ask For Wisdom?

1. To enjoy prosperity, long life, honor and wealth. (In her right hand wisdom holds a long life and in her left hand are wealth and honor. Prov. 3:16 CEV)
2. To have a good life. Wisdom makes life pleasant and leads us safely along. Prov. 3:17 CEV

3. To enjoy vitality and happiness. Wisdom is a life-giving tree, the source of happiness for all who hold on to her. Prov. 3:18 CEV

4. To be sure of protection. You will walk safely and never stumble. Prov. 3:23 CEV

5. To experience a refreshing rest. You will rest without a worry and sleep soundly. Prov. 3:24 CEV

6. To obtain confidence. You can be sure that the LORD will protect you from harm. Prov. 3:26 CEV

7. To know safety. If you love Wisdom and don't reject her, she will watch over you. Prov. 4:6 CEV

8. To receive promotion. If you value Wisdom and hold tightly to her; great honors will be yours.   Prov. 4:8 CEV

9. To receive protection. Wisdom will control your mind and you will be pleased with knowledge. Sound judgment and good sense will watch over you. Wisdom will protect you from evil schemes and from

those liars who turned from doing good to live in the darkness. Prov. 2: 10-13 CEV

10. To get knowledge. If you are already wise, you will become wiser. Prov. 1:5 CEV

This is the Touch of God's Grace. I hope you receive a very special blessing today! Shalom!

It's A New Day

The steadfast love of the LORD never ceases; his mercies never come to an end; they are new every morning; great is your faithfulness. Lam. 3:22 - 23 ESV

We have the tendency to take every day for granted. The sun came up yesterday and it will come up again tomorrow. That's the way the world is. Why give thanks for something that is so predictable? Because we deceive ourselves by thinking that each day will be the same.

In reality, today is a new day. It is a gift for God. No day is the same as the previous one any other one, and no day in the future will be the same as another.

To me, this is a sign of hope. My reserve for faith, hope and love is limited and it is exhausted easily. Sometimes I go to bed very tired, without the most minimal drop of energy or emotion, desiring only to forget in my sleep. But with God's marvelous grace, he uses the hours of darkness and the time of slumber to restore me completely. In the morning, I wake up with new energy, ready for new opportunities, new experiences and new encounters with other people. Who knows what God will do with this new day? Remember, "Every morning His mercies are new."

When you awaken, declare a new mercy for yourself, your loved ones, and for the community where you live. Everything we declare with our mouth, that will we receive.

Today Lord, I declare that your mercies that you have prepared for all who have believed in you, will fall on the place where we inhabit, work and live. Because your mercies are new every morning, I can hope on big things with your favor and your mercy.

Thank you Lord for your love, so undeserved!

Surrender to God Every Day

What happens in a marriage when one spouse does not listen to the other? The answer is: after a short time, bitterness starts to enter into the heart. The words begin to cut like a sharp knife. Soon after, hostility becomes anger, jealousy and even worse emotions. For many, the solution is separation, then divorce and hatred.

However, this disconnect can be mended easily. All that is needed is a fresh surrender that comes straight from the soul. The renewal that, "You will love, honor and care for one another until death will separate you."

This same thing happens when you neglect the Lord. You feel bitterness and hatred. All of a sudden, you fall away from the communion with the Lord. That is what happened to the children of Israel in the wilderness. (NUM. 14:2-3 CEV) *We wish we had died in Egypt or somewhere out here in the dessert! Is the Lord leading us into Canaan, just to have us killed and our women and children captured? We'd be better off in Egypt.* And the Lord said to Moses and Aaron, "*How long will these foolish people complain about me?*"

The children of Israel stopped saying, "The Lord is God," but complained saying, "It's better to go back to Egypt." What caused this change? They stopped searching for the Lord and their hearts hardened. Before they were able to understand what was happening, they left Him. We must not let one day pass without a fresh surrender to the Lord. We must never give up. Our bodies are gradually dying, but we ourselves are being made stronger each day. (II. COR. 4:16)

The surrender has to be continuous, and interminable emptying of ourselves before the Lord. When it is done habitually, we will experience the perfect union, the perfect communion, the perfect understanding and the perfect love. This perfection will dismiss all of our fears and we will be able to forgive trespasses committed by others and by ourselves.

Today, I surrender to you my Lord. Forgive my debts as I forgive the debts that others have committed against me. In Jesus' name, Amen.

But what does it say? "The word is near you, in your mouth and in your heart" (that is, the word of faith that we proclaim); because, if you confess with your mouth that Jesus is Lord and believe in your heart that God raised him from the dead, you will be saved. Romans 10: 8-9

What we think determines our beliefs. If we think bad, we believe bad. The word of God is given to us to correct our way of thinking. If our beliefs are wrong, our confession will be wrong too. In other words, our words will be wrong as a result of our way of thinking.

Jesus said in Mark 11: 23, *"If you have faith in God and don't doubt, you can tell this mountain to get up and jump into the sea, and it will.* We talk too much about believing, but we don't say enough. Certainly we cannot speak correctly until we begin to think correctly. Our way of thinking has to be according to the Word of God. We will only believe what we know that is in God's word.

"*Trust the Lord with all your heart and not your own judgment.* (Prov. 3:5 CEV)

"*Casting down imaginations and every high thing that exalted itself against the knowledge of God and bring into captivity every thought to the obedience of Christ.* (II. COR. 10:5 ASV)

Do not be conformed to this world, but be transformed by the renewing of your mind, that you may prove what is that good and acceptable and perfect will of God. (ROM. 12:2 KJV)

The study of the word of God renews the mind. It teaches us to have the mind of Christ, believing with the heart and doing what the word says. The word of God also teaches us to think every good thing, pure and honest, and if there is virtue in it.

Would you like to have the mind of Christ and think good things that are pure and honest? Find a good church where you can study the word of God. Your mind will be changed. The way you speak will change and God will use you to take others to the level where God has taken you, because God had known you and He has known your thoughts.

"For I know the plans I have for you, declares the Lord. Plans to prosper you and not to harm you. Plans to give you hope and a future. (JER. 29:11 TLB)

In the State of Florida, there are insects known as fire ants. These diminutive creatures build ant hills in patios and gardens. Sometimes, when we work in the garden, we can feel their sting. But when we apply a special medicine, the pain goes away and the sting heals in a few days.

Sometimes our lives are like the experience with the fire ants. We go about our day-to-day routine, we do housework, schoolwork, ministries at church and tasks on our jobs until surprisingly, we are stung by some irritating situation. It can happen when we drive our cars in traffic, in relationships with our co-workers, with neighbors and even with family members. What can alleviate our pain and make us feel better?

Only the grace of God in our lives can help. When we treasure in our heart His message and experience His love, we feel the peace and assurance of our God. It does not matter what the situation, misunderstanding and or bad intention of those who tend to irritate us. It is easier to respond kindly as Jesus did when he faced the Pharisees, who did not understand that truly He was the son of God and that He came to this earth with a mission to restore the humanity in those who were lost.

The life of Jesus is the best example of the grace of God. We could say that the grace of God was personified in the life of Christ. In His words, in His nobility and in His simple character, full of authority.

The Grace of God helped Jesus to walk between the Pharisees, doing what the Father had commanded Him to do. Jesus taught us , His followers, that only His grace can help us to carry out that which God has called us to do. Filled with meekness, nobility, humility, holiness and much peace, we will be able to get to those who are lonely, sad, and discouraged in life, and teach them the peace that transcends all understanding. The grace of God will help us to be loving, even in difficult times, with people who need to receive the divine grace to be more than conquerors in their struggles.

May the grace of God help you to be more than conquerors in this life as Jesus prophesized over those who will treasure His words and His love.

The craving of a sluggard will be the death of him because his hands refuse to work. Proverbs 21: 25 (NIV)

To earn the bread of each day with the "sweat from your face" could be a divine curse because of the sin committed by our first fathers. But like all punishments inflicted by God, it has a final good purpose.

When we are busy in the struggle for survival, we are less exposed to the temptations than those who are idle. Proverbs 10:4 says, "*A slack hand causes poverty, but the hand of the diligent makes rich.*" We all dream with prosperity and economic security, but the idle do not have the disposition to reach out with determination. His idle mind is filled with great plans. Could he know how to proceed to bring to reality his ambitious plans? But his hands do not want to work.

The situation of Israel in the days of Gideon were dark. The Midianites crossed the borders of the land and they looted all the crops. The perspectives were discouraging, but Gideon continued working diligently, tilling the earth, storing the grain and hiding it from the greed of the invaders. That's why he was chosen by the hand of God to free the people from the Midianite yoke. God is never going to us a lazy person or an idle person for His service. The scriptures and history confirmed this truth with countless examples of callings that God directed to laborious men.

Moses was busy with his herds in Mount Horeb when God called him. Saul was determined to find his father's lost donkey when God called him. Eliseo was working in the fields when the Lord found him. Nehemiah was at the service of the king when God challenged him to build a national restoration. Peter and Andrew were throwing their nets into the sea when Jesus invited them to follow Him. Matthew was collecting taxes due to Caesar when Jesus called him to be one of the Apostles.

Remember today that God created men and settled him in the garden of Eden to cultivate and care for it. (GEN. 2:15)

Those who work their land will have abundant food, but those who chase fantasies will have their fill of poverty. (PROV. 28:19)

They do not need to go away, you give them something to eat. (MATT. 14:16 (NIV)

During a whole day, Jesus comforted the whole crowd with His compassionate teachings. The shadows of the night started to descend over the earth and the disciples did not hide their fears. The people have not been fed. How can they feed so many people? How will they face this situation? With fear they suggested to the Lord, "Send them away, that they may go into the country round about and into the villages and buy themselves something to eat." (MAR 3:36 NIV)

The attitude of the disciples is unbelievable. Engrossed in His labor, Jesus was concerned for the spiritual needs of the crowd. Like a flock without a pastor, they needed someone who would lead them towards the green pastures of the Gospel. The disciples, however, had their own concerns towards the physical needs of the people. However, Jesus, like the diligent pastor He is, was not indifferent to their physical needs even in the midst of caring for their spiritual needs.

Replying to his scared disciples, he commanded, "Give them something to eat." Surprised, with sharp discernment, Phillip replied, "It would take more than half a year's wages to buy enough bread for each of them to have one bite." Poor disciple! He ignored the Creator's power and it seems that his trust was based on the power of money and not in the power of God.

From the human viewpoint, the divine commandment was unreasonable. However, He who, in the beginning of the darkness, created the light, and from the chaos created the cosmos, could deed the crowd. Yes, the same God who supplied Israel with manna in the desert, orchestrated a great miracle, multiplying five loaves of bread and two fish with such grace that the whole crowd was thoroughly fed.

We live in a hungry world. There are millions of human beings sick and underfed, who live in miserable conditions, without any perspective of better days. However, worse than physical hunger, there is the spiritual hunger that was described by the Prophet Amos. *"Behold, the day shall come, saith the Lord, that I will send a famine in the land, not a famine of bread, not a thirst of water, but of hearing the Words of the Lord."* There are great crowds that parish without Christ, the Bread of Life.

In a time as this, Lets hear with a new meaning and profound, divine command, the Word of God: GIVE THEM SOMETHING TO EAT!

Pastors: GIVE THEM SOMETHING TO EAT!

Missionaries: GIVE THEM SOMETHING TO EAT!

Evangelists: GIVE THEM SOMETHING TO EAT!

Brothers who understand that the great commission to take the bread of life is for all who have believed and have eaten from this bread, give them something to eat! Now, when there is so much need and those who do not know that the Lord can satisfy all needs, both naturally and physically: GIVE THEM SOMETHING TO EAT, saith the Lord.

"What is that in your hand? A staff he replied." EXODUS. 4:2

Moses was feeding the sheep in the sunny mountains of Midian when his attention was called by a bush that was burning, yet not consumed. He came closer to examine it, when he heard the voice of the Great I AM calling him by his name. Immediately, he hid his face for he was afraid to look upon God. Afterwards, there was a conversation between God and the Pastor of Midian.

"What is that in your hand?" the Lord asked.

"A staff," he replied.

From this memorable conversation, it turned out to be an order to Moses to go back to Egypt, and with the staff, free his people. The biblical account says that Moses obeyed and with his staff, he made signs and wonders.

Today we ask, "What do you have in your hand?"

David had a slingshot and five stones and in the power of God, he killed Goliath and saved the Israelites from becoming slaves to the Philistines.

A woman, Mary Magdalene, had an alabaster bottle of very expensive ointment, and with that she anointed Jesus for his burial.

Lutero the Reformer, had a document where he gathered ninety five reasons to oppose indulgence, looking at the door of his church, indicated a movement that changed the current history.

What do you have in your hand?

On that night that Jesus was betrayed, He took a towel and girded himself. After which, he poured water into a basin and began to wash the feet of his disciples. Yes, in that distressed hour, Jesus had in his hand a towel, a symbol of the unselfish service he demonstrated to his fellow man. The majesty of heaven inclined humbly to teach us a great lesson of service.

Let's take today in our hands, "the towel" and with humility, let's serve our neighbors and those who need our help. Amen.

MY TESTIMONY

THE GRACE OF GOD IN MY LIFE

The Grace of God came to my life the 5th day of July at 7 o'clock in the morning when a Sun ray (Celestial Light) entered into the bedroom and touched me at the moment of my birth to the Rivera Family in La Playa de Ponce, Puerto Rico. The Midwife that was helping my mother to bring me into this world, when she saw the Sun ray come into the room through the small opening from the wall of that old house, was very surprised and told my mother, "Name this child Luz because I think she is going to be a light in the midst of the darkness for many".

That was a prophecy to us without anybody realizing it at that moment. They named me Luz and since that beautiful and sunny day I was marked for the Ministry of Service to the needy. That became my purpose and my mission in my life and in this world from that moment. It is a mission that I carried through the years, serving in different jobs like in the Help

Ministries in Harrisburg, PA since 2019 (Christian Churches United Ministry to help the needy). I have also worked in different churches where I have served as a Missionary . In the community of Tampa, Florida, I served for 12 years in the community to assist needy families through the Department of Juvenile Justice, the place where I retired in 2012.

As I was growing, I started to understand in my heart that God had called me to serve Him through serving every person in need. I understood the meaning of His words in Matthew 25:40: "*The King will reply, Truly I tell you, whatever you did for one of the least of these brothers and sisters, you did for me*". And through God's word, I realized the purpose of my life. God opened the doors for this ministry in me every time that I needed a job and in every place where there was a needy person or family.

I was married for 29 years until my husband passed away with the Lord in the year 2022. I have two children, Willie and Janie Luz. Seven grandchildren, Kaitilyn Luz, Misael, Jazmine, Blayze, Ciara, Desiree and Mariah, and three great-grandchildren, Esme Luz, Katai and Rheyna. All of them are precious to me. I love them with all my heart and I consider them my biggest treasure in this life. Children are the biggest blessing that comes from the Lord!

I feel so grateful and thankful because God always has taken care of me with an eternal love, even when He had to discipline me, when I disobeyed Him. He has done it to show me His great love for me as He does for all His creation.

I treasure the grace of God and His mercy because it is the most valuable experience that has happened to me in my life. Without it, I probably would not have obtained anything in this life and who knows where I would be. In His word/touch of God's grace, God has written in my heart, I have found a shelter that gives me comfort in times of mourning and also gives me joy in times of peace.

Solomon with his wisdom which He asked God to give him, teaches us the times of the Lord in our lives:

A time to be born and a time to die; a time to plant and a time to pluck up that which is planted. A time to kill and a time to heal; a time to break down and a time to build up. A time to weep and a time to laugh; a time to mourn and a time to dance. A time to cast away stones and a time to gather stones. A time to embrace and a time to refrain from embracing. A time to get and a time to lose; a time to keep and a time to cast away. A time to rend and a time to sew; a time to keep silence and a time to speak. A time to love and a time to hate. A time of war and a time of Peace. Ecclesiastes 3:1-15

Solomon sends a warning in these amazing words that we need to take advantage of the time that God gives us to live and find the purpose of why we came to the world because we do not know when will be the time that we must return to our creator. That which has been, is now, and that which is to be, has already been. God restores that which is past. I give God all the glory and all the honor for all of my life and until eternity.

God is good all the time.   II. Cor. 12:9